THE UNCANCELLED MANDATE

Four Bible Studies
on Christian Mission
for the Approaching Millennium

John V. Taylor

Board of Mission Occasional Paper No. 8

CHURCH HOUSE
PUBLISHING

In gratitude to fellow workers and friends
in the Church Mission Society
as we celebrate together its bicentenary

Church House Publishing
Great Smith Street,
London SW1P 3NZ

ISBN 0 7151 5541 5

First published in 1998 by Church House Publishing

This series of addresses, given at a Retreat for the Partnership for World Mission Committee, does not constitute an authoritative statement of the General Synod of the Church of England. It is published by the Board of Mission to encourage study and discussion.

Printed in England by Halstan & Co. Ltd, Amersham, Bucks

Contents

Foreword   iv

Preface   v

Acknowledgements   vi

1   God's mission   1

2   God's partners   11

3   God's temple   22

4   God's time   31

Foreword

Bishop John V. Taylor, former Bishop of Winchester and General Secretary of the Church Missionary Society, is one of our most distinguished missionary statesmen. It was, therefore, a great privilege for the General Secretaries of the Church of England's world mission agencies and other members of the Partnership for World Mission Committee to listen to his reflections on mission at a retreat we held in March 1997. It was our unanimous view that they should be made available to a wider audience.

These four studies are the fruit of a lifetime of prayer and study, experience and reflection. In the midst of the many pressing issues of life, which can so catch us up in immediate concerns, they recall us to basic truths – the love and ultimate purposes of God, revealed in Jesus Christ, and the requirement of a response by humankind in the present. They are informed by Bishop Taylor's profound understanding of the Scriptures.

This small book is one which should be read and reread by anyone concerned with Christian mission at the present time. It is particularly significant for those in any position of leadership in the Church. I am happy and honoured to commend it.

† *Patrick Southwell*
Chair, Partnership for World Mission

Preface

The following chapters are a slight adaptation of four talks which I have given for several different groups of people during the past years. Three of them formed the basis of a retreat for the committee members of Partnership for World Mission in the spring of 1997.

They are no more than one man's attempt to clarify the fundamental basis and objective of the Christian mission at this moment when the approaching millennium, as well as the centenaries of several of the British mission agencies, are compelling us all to take stock, look backwards and forwards and, if necessary, change direction.

As I am no longer in touch with the organizational questions and the technical issues that are the daily concerns of national churches and mission agencies, my approach may strike anyone with executive responsibility as naive and uninformed. Nevertheless I believe that the purpose of God and the call of Christ do not change, though our perception of them and the means we employ may do so. So I have simply taken the three terms which define the area of our corporate Christian obedience – 'world mission', 'partnership' and 'the Church', and also 'time' because of the particular pressures of this moment, and have tried to reformulate the theological insight underlying each of them. Each chapter, therefore, is basically a simple Bible study.

The words of Scripture, therefore, are printed in italics with the Bible references inserted either after each verse or, when several follow in succession, in a group at the end of the paragraph. The text, unless otherwise identified, is that of either the New English Bible or its later revision, the Revised English Bible. Verses indicated by an asterisk are the author's own translation or have been amended by him.

I am very grateful to John Clark, Secretary of PWM, for inviting me to offer these talks for publication, and to his Personal Assistant, Sally Smith, for transforming my manuscript and subsequent alterations into a publishable text.

Acknowledgements

The publisher gratefully acknowledges permission to reproduce copyright material in this book. Every effort has been made to trace and contact copyright holders. If there are any inadvertent omissions we apologise to those concerned and will ensure that a suitable acknowledgement is made at the next reprint.

New English Bible © Oxford University Press and Cambridge University Press 1961, 1970.

Revised English Bible © Oxford University Press and Cambridge University Press 1989.

The Authorized (King James) Version. Rights in the Authorized Version are vested in the Crown. Reproduced by permission of the Crown's patentee, Cambridge University Press.

The Revised Standard Version of the Bible © 1952 and 1971 National Council of the Churches of Christ in the USA.

The image of Jonah from the Sistine Chapel ceiling (cover illustration) is copyright © Monumenti Musei e Gallerie Pontificie Città del Vaticano 1993.

Cover illustration

This shows the upper half of the figure of the prophet Jonah painted by Michelangelo as one item in his great design for the vault of the Sistine Chapel in Rome. It is placed in the central panel against the east wall immediately above the high altar. Its sharply twisted posture shows God's reluctant messenger being called back to go in the opposite direction to the one he has chosen to take.

The word of the Lord came to Jonah son of Amittai: 'Go to the great city of Nineveh, go now . . .'

But Jonah set out for Tarshish to escape from the Lord . . .

The word of the Lord came to Jonah a second time: 'Go to the great city of Nineveh, go now . . .'

(Jonah 1.1,2; 1.3; 3.1,2)

1

God's mission

The history of religion is full of ironies which, if we could not laugh at them as Jesus seems to have done, would indeed be tragic. Christians, for example, like to point out that it was when their divided Churches had taken up again the task of sharing their faith worldwide through the missionary movement of recent centuries that the road to reunion began to open up. The ecumenical movement was born from the Missionary Conference at Edinburgh in 1910.

And yet – here comes the irony – separated Churches have developed different ideologies and styles. Only let all the congregations in one town, or all the chaplains in one university, agree to organize a special Mission or a Decade of Evangelism, and they may spend a year arguing what they mean by the word! In other great traditions, notably the Orthodox Churches, the very concept of mission is suspect, being identified with proselytism and sheep-stealing; while comparatively new branches of the historic Churches, which now comprise the majority of Christians in the world, associate 'missions' with a past dependency on some expatriate presence. By mid-century, in the name of their own authenticity, the cry was being raised: 'Missionary, go home!'

The flourishing ecumenical movement, reluctant to turn its own mother from the door, was in a dilemma. It resolved its embarrassment by coining the gloriously inclusive term 'The Mission of God', thereby in one stroke expanding the concept beyond any narrowly specific form or objective, while ensuring its continuance since, if it be God's Mission, it is not for any of us to call it off.

But the point was won at a very significant cost. For there is an inherent, if not deliberate, vagueness in the term 'Mission of God' which lays it open to abuse. It can be made to include anything under the sun that anyone considers a Good Thing. It is a title to which various conflicting ideologies have laid claim. No doubt those in the churches who favoured the term were hoping, and with good reason, to broaden the popular perception of what the word 'mission' might include. But I believe they were confusing the particular scope of the Christian mission, however broad that might be, with the vast inclusiveness of the ultimate purpose of God for the creation. They were confusing the divine means with the divine end. For the mission that has been laid upon the Christian community from its inception arose out of, and is forever focused upon, the historical event of Jesus Christ and the task he believed he was sent to undertake as the means of bringing the purposes of God to fruition.

Just consider how the word 'mission' is used in common parlance. A diplomatic mission is the delegation sent to a particular situation on a long- or short-term assignment to further the political or economic goals of the sending state. A trade mission likewise undertakes a business errand to forward the plans of particular companies. A space mission, whether manned or simply mechanical, goes to carry forward some defined part of a vast integrated programme, a programme of space exploration or communications development. In every case the mission *serves* a wider purpose and plan. It is the sending of a particular group of experts to do a particular thing in a particular place *for the sake of a wider plan*. Those engaged on the mission may know very little about that, but the most responsible missions are probably the most informed about the purpose behind them.

What about the Christian mission? Behind the Christian mission, behind the mission of Christ, lies the purpose of God insofar as we can ever presume to penetrate that mystery. That is what should determine all our thinking about the mission. 'Goals', wrote Thomas Aquinas, 'are more valuable than means to goals,' and he applied that insight especially to God's relationship to his creation.

God's planning of the universe, he said, is called his providence. This planning or providence is eternal though its implementation and management takes place in time. It was St Paul's claim that through the coming of Christ God's eternal purpose for the creation, formerly only dimly perceived by human minds, had been made clear. *I speak*, says St Paul, *God's hidden wisdom, his secret purpose framed from the very beginning to bring us to our full glory.* (1 Corinthians 2.7)

It took the Church two and a half centuries to formulate what he meant by that, but briefly we can put it in these terms. God is love – hence God's very being, unlike ours, is within itself a dynamic flow and exchange of relationships. God is communion – what Chesterton called 'the dance of the Three in One'. How else could he be love? But God is love and love means self-giving; hence the eternal purpose of this triune God to share existence with what did not exist, and response with what could not respond. God wanted to bring into being some other, apart from the divine Self, which had those qualities of existence and response.

The universe is God's 'Other' upon which his love is working to bring it to the capacity of making its free, conscious response of love, mirroring his own love. That is what St Paul called 'bringing us to our full glory' – the evolution of consciousness, response and love.

That, we believe, is the originating Idea and Purpose of the eternal love, and that idea and purpose is what theologically we name the Father. It is the Idea, the vision, the possibility of fulfilling that purpose that is the source of it all.

The active Expression of that Idea which is the next stage in creation, embodying it perfectly in form and substance in obedience to that purpose, is what we name the Son. Don't imagine that this obedience must imply two quite separate wills or minds. In our own experience as creators we form an idea and immediately we are under an obligation. Once we have conceived the idea in the first place, we then feel: 'Now I *must* carry it out.' So it is, we may say, within the mind of God. For it is the Son who goes forth, as it were, from within the being of God to give being and form to God's idea and desire, giving it flesh and blood, like the director of a supreme dramatist's play, bringing it into conscious, freely-given response to God's love for it. That is the mission of God the Son to the end of time. So we can properly speak of the mission of Christ, or the mission of God the Son.

3

And what we might call the delighted Recognition of the worth of the Idea and of its emerging Expression, the divine 'Oh yes!', which burns in God's patience and kindles our awareness, that is what we call Holy Spirit, the giver of our awareness towards anything that is in accordance with God's love. 'Oh yes!'

These three distinct yet inseparable aspects of creative love are implicitly presented in the Genesis account of the first day of creation (Genesis 1.3,4). *God said, 'Let there be light'* – the Idea. And then the obedient execution of the Idea, *and there was light*. And at once the recognition of its worth. *God saw that the light was good.* 'Oh yes!'

Can you see now why it is more helpful, because more exact, to talk about the mission of God the Son or the mission of Christ coupled with the mission of the Spirit? It proclaims the essential element of obedience, of being under obligation, of carrying out a commission, of being sent, of serving a fixed purpose. It also helps us to bear in mind the *exemplary principle* which Scripture reveals as the perennial method by which the eternal Word and Wisdom, God the Son, has been bringing the Idea and Purpose of the Father towards its fuller completion.

By the *exemplary* method I mean the vocation of a part to pioneer the way forward for the whole. Let's start with a part and bring it forward so that the rest can follow. The break-up of humanity into separate cultures and histories is in the book of Genesis the prelude to the call of Abraham, the father of the People of God, that People who shall be blessed in order to be a blessing to the rest. And what a blessing the object lesson of Jewish response to God has been! *These events happened*, says St Paul, *as symbols to warn us*. (1 Corinthians 10.6) I cannot help feeling embarrassed by such a cavalier usurpation of the blessings that have flowed from Jewish history, but we can let that pass. All humanity becomes the heir to the formative experiences of each particular culture, and that fact underlies what I call God's exemplary method.

Yet the Jewish demonstration of response to God's love was, we must admit, only partial, as ours in our turn as Christians has been. Theirs was not only flawed by occasional apostasy, falling back into idolatry,

4

but it remained too narrowly self-interested. They forgot about being a blessing to the others. For example, Isaiah magnificently proclaims:

> *The LORD of Hosts has sworn:*
> *In very truth, as I planned, so shall it be;*
> *as I designed, so shall it fall out . . .*

The Idea and then the Expression.

> *This is the plan prepared for the whole earth,*
> *this the hand stretched out over all the nations.*
>
> (Isaiah 14.24,26)

But when he specifies what divine purpose he is talking about, it turns out to be no more than the breaking of the Assyrian hold over the little kingdom of Judah. Before we too quickly condemn that narrow concept of God's purpose we should ask ourselves whether our own Christian perception of it is still large enough to be true.

To counter such narrow self-concern and in order that people might grasp the full scope of his eternal purpose God paradoxically narrowed his use of the exemplary principle. The task of demonstrating what a perfect response to God's love might be was transferred from the People of God to the Son of God.

God the Son, ever obedient to the originating Idea and Purpose, gave final Expression and substance to it in the perfect response of one human life. Through the human consciousness and through the human prayer of Jesus, we hear one side of the eternal communication of the Three in One: '*my aim is not my own will, but the will of him who sent me.*' (John 5.30) Those words are not just the words of Jesus of Nazareth. They are his words as a human, but what they express is the eternal attitude and obedience of God the Son within the triune God: 'I must give expression to the Idea, give form to the Plan.'

But from that narrowing down of the divine purpose to its fulfilment in one perfectly responsive life St Paul saw an expansion, a vast blossoming out, which he envisaged taking place at three levels.

First, at the level of personal confrontation, which was his own experience, Paul speaks of God's hidden purpose being fulfilled as individuals are made one, as he had been, in mind and spirit with Jesus Christ and his total response of sonship towards the Father. The Spirit, he writes,

> *co-operates for good with those who love God and are called according to his purpose. For God knew his own before ever they were, and also ordained that they should be shaped to the likeness of his Son, that he might be the eldest among a large family of brothers and sisters.*
>
> (Romans 8.28-9★)

So, says St Paul (Ephesians 1.6), God's high favour has been *conferred on us in his Beloved.* The same term is used by the angel when he calls Mary 'the *favoured one*' (Luke 1.28 RSV). Therein lies our sonship of God. This concept of the extension of the one responding Son of God underlies Paul's great doctrine of being 'in Christ', of being the Body of Christ. He speaks in Colossians 1.25-7 of *the task assigned to me by God . . . to announce the secret hidden for long ages and through many generations, but now disclosed to God's people . . . The secret is this: Christ in you together, the hope of a glory to come.* (I've put in the word 'together' because we've so often taken it as though it's in the singular, but it's a plural in the Greek.) Christ in you - in between you, in your one-anotherness - the hope of glory to come, the hope of your final fulfilment and that of all creation.

And if you regard that passage from Colossians as post-Pauline, then take this definition of his mission from his unquestioned early epistle to the Galatians. *My little children, with whom I am again in travail until Christ be formed in you!* (Galatians 4.19 RSV) Nor is the idea exclusively St Paul's, for it is given its ultimate expression in the high-priestly prayer of Jesus in the Gospel of John (17.22-3): *The glory which thou gavest me* (that is, God the Son) *I have given to them,* your Son, *that they may be one, as we are one; I in them and thou in me, may they be perfectly one* – one in perfection.

The second level on which Paul saw the fulfilment of God's eternal purpose as an expansion of the perfect response that Jesus had offered as Son of God was the cultural and historical level. In his personal obedience Jesus had been the true Israel. That Israel was now ready to fulfil the role committed to Abraham to extend his blessedness to all peoples. So Paul writes to the Ephesians, *I understand the secret of Christ. In former generations this was not disclosed to the human race; but now it has been revealed by inspiration to his dedicated apostles and prophets, that through the Gospel the Gentiles are joint heirs with the Jews* . . . (Ephesians 3.4–6) There is the expansion culturally: not just the Jewish way of looking at things, the Jewish way of understanding God; now they were going to embrace other ways as part of the same Body, sharers together in God's promise in Christ Jesus.

We must never forget that this expansion of the Abrahamic promise to the Abrahamic People of God was clearly envisaged by Paul not as absorption into the culture and history of Judaism, as the Old Testament prophets had imagined, but as an opening up, by a mutual sharing of what in the same passage he calls *the wisdom of God in all its varied forms* – a mutual sharing above all in the perfect human response to God offered by Jesus once for all – *God's age-long purpose, which he achieved in Christ Jesus Our Lord.* (Ephesians 3.11) This is the cultural level of the fulfilment we should look for. Have we faced that as Christians? It may be as hard for us as it was for the Jews.

And the third level on which St Paul saw the realization of the eternal purpose blossoming out from that one perfect offering of responsive love is a cosmic level which our minds can scarcely grasp. In our own day Teilhard de Chardin and a few others have tried to put it into words, but I don't feel they make it as compelling as Paul's daring vision.

> *God has made known to us his secret purpose, in accordance with the plan which he determined beforehand in Christ, to be put into effect when the time was ripe: namely, that the universe, everything in heaven and on earth, might be brought into a unity in Christ.*
>
> (Ephesians 1.9–10)

The creation itself, drawn up within God the Son into the flow and exchange of the eternal love, yet remaining for ever God's 'Other', God's adopted child.

This heavy dose of rather speculative theology may seem quite remote from the practical decisions and the working relationships which must be the daily concern of anyone engaged in the mission of the Church in the world. Yet I make no apology, for I believe that strategy must be based on a clear grasp of the ultimate objective. So I will attempt to end this chapter by showing how our mission, which is still essentially Christ's mission, in adapting to the new features in the world situation, can best be guided, not by *ad hoc* tactical reactions to events, but by reference back to that unchanging purpose which the mission is meant to serve. To take a simple example first, urgent ecological issues are clearly on the agenda of any preview of the years ahead, and poorer nations are scared lest it be their development that is sacrificed to limit the damage. A divine purpose that embraces the physical processes of our planet in its scope, 'everything in heaven and on earth', is the strongest possible mandate for the universal call for reverent care in place of greedy exploitation and continuous economic growth. And the burden must be carried by those nations which are most excessive in their exploitation and their expectations of growth.

These, then, are some of the other most significant changes to which Christian mission must respond as we look to the end of this century and the start of the next millennium.

1. Christianity's centre of gravity, its natural base, both numerical and dynamic, has now moved from its European and North American heartlands to Latin America, Africa and the Pacific. Culturally and economically this is a change no less radical than the early Church's migration from Jerusalem to the Graeco-Roman cities in the first century when Christianity ceased to be Jewish; or equally the change from a centripetal, consolidated Christendom to a centrifugal, dispersed Christianity in the sixteenth century.

2. For the first time in a millennium the Church is the Church of the poor - not *for* the poor - *of* the poor. That hasn't been the case for a thousand years. But if you look at the areas of the globe where the majority of Christians live and worship you will see that they are not a rich Church. They are not - let's say, we are not - a Church of the powerful people of the world.

3. The failure of Communism in all but a few countries, so far from leaving the Capitalist system as undisputed favourite, has cleared

the way for the world to see its moral defects. It could get along without our noticing these as long as we were fighting Communism. Now there is no enemy, we can turn and look at ourselves and we can see how totally inadequate the Capitalist system is, morally. Its immense power is no longer seen as the natural ally to the spread of any of the world's religions, but rather as a system to be challenged by them.

4. The realities of a religiously pluralist world are compelling us all to re-examine our former terms of approach to the adherents of other faiths. In many situations we meet them now as fellow fighters for the same moral and spiritual values, standing together on the same side, and so, as colleagues, a little more ready to hear what we have to say to each other – they to us and we to them.

5. The single issue that will threaten to divide not only Christians but adherents of other faiths also for some time to come is the rift between those who consider that in matters of belief and religious practice the content and meaning is paramount, while the forms in which it is conveyed are variable, and those who hold that a particular form is essential to guarantee that the content is unchanged.

What manner of mission then will best serve the eternal purpose of God to draw humanity into the perfect response of his Son at this unfolding moment? That must be our question; may I just offer two pointers?

The primary aim of all Christian mission in all its varied activities is to present the person of Jesus Christ, to make *him* visible, to lift *him* up, as he truly was and is, so that *he* rather than anything else we bring may draw all to himself. I don't see that any other than that can be obedience to the purpose as I have tried to describe it.

Our definitions of him – definitions arrived at in our Classical European past – may never touch the minds or hearts of people with a different culture or religion. But what if they could start afresh, as it were, as the disciples of Jesus did from within Judaism, and then wrestle with his meaning amid the presuppositions of their own backgrounds, just as Christians in Europe in the midst of Greek philosophy and Roman organization wrestled with this strange experience that had come from Palestine? But first they must *see* him in his humanity, and that can only be in the Christ-likeness of other human beings and in a Church that actually *is* his Body. I would like to place on the desk of every mission executive, not least those concerned with aid and development, and in all centres of training mission partners, a card bearing the words, 'Sirs, we would <u>see</u> Jesus' with the verb underlined. Simplistic? Certainly. But it might serve as a corrective to a Church which, in the words of a recent book review, 'trusts administrators more than saints and working parties above prophets'.

And then secondly, if the essence of mission is the charge laid upon all churches to re-present Jesus Christ and his total response to the Father, we need a scrupulous reappraisal of the connection between inter-church partnership in mission and the huge economic disparity of the partners. The care and championship of the disadvantaged, even on a large institutional scale, can rightly be termed a Christ-like activity, and many have seen Jesus truly revealed in figures like Helda Camara, Mother Teresa, Jean Vanier - though the mention of such names prompts the thought that all of them came very close to sharing the poverty of the poor they served.

Again, our enormously larger resources of money and technology may help to augment and equip our partner churches for their own mission, yet those riches are not necessarily the best contribution we have to offer them. Too much dependence on them may only perpetuate the imbalance which now distorts our partnership. We need to think long and hard about the word 'development'. It begs too many questions, assuming that the developed nations are the paradigm-model that the rest are bound to emulate, until all have become clones of our Euro-American society and its values. We in the Christian mission have a different model in view - one in which the rich heritage of every culture will be honoured and gathered up in one.

Partnership between Churches in mission means also an apostolic concern from one to the other to help one another to present the likeness of Christ more clearly; being in travail one for another until we all are formed in the shape of Christ. Which partners, I wonder, do we naturally cast in the parental role of St Paul? And which are the Galatians now?

2

God's partners

A significant pointer to the meaning of partnership is one of the stories from St John's Gospel (chapter 5). It begins with a miracle which is also a sign (vv. 1-9): *Later on Jesus went up to Jerusalem for one of the Jewish festivals.* We've no clear indication which festival it was, but the most detailed weighing of the evidence, which is Bishop Lightfoot's, suggests it might have been the Day of Atonement, Yom Kippur. Little points later in the story suggest that that is probably right.

Now at the Sheep-Pool in Jerusalem there is a place with five colonnades. Its name in the language of the Jews is Bethesda. In these colonnades there lay a crowd of sick people, blind, lame, and paralysed. And, if you are interested, there is some dispute as to the original version of that name – that it might have been Beth-hesedha which means 'The House of faithful Mercy'. Excavations at the traditional site to the north of the Temple area in Jerusalem have shown that in the period of Roman Jerusalem in the second century AD there was a healing sanctuary there above a cluster of natural cisterns in the limestone rock. And Josephus wrote about intermittent springs in that district at the time of the Siege of Jerusalem in AD 69.

For us, though, the significant words in this introductory description of the setting for the miracle are 'a crowd of sick people, blind, lame and paralysed'. For these at many points in the Gospels represent humanity in its helplessness, in its need of divine intervention. They are the ones, according to Jesus, whom we should invite to our parties, the crippled, the lame and the blind. They are the ones whom the host in the parable brought in from the streets and alleys of the town when the guests who were first invited failed to turn up. They represent one permanent facet of what is happening in the world, namely humanity's

11

perennial blindness and impotence. And it is their healing that demon-
strates the arrival of the Saviour-God promised by the prophets.

> *Strengthen the feeble arms,*
> *steady the tottering knees;*
> *say to the anxious, Be strong and fear not.*
> *See, your God comes with vengeance* (to avenge you),
> *with dread retribution he comes to save you.*
> *Then shall blind men's eyes be opened,*
> *and the ears of the deaf unstopped.*
> *Then shall the lame man leap like a deer,*
> *and the tongue of the dumb shout aloud . . .*

(Isaiah 35.3-6)

And so when Jesus received John the Baptist's message, '*Are you the one
who is to come, or are we to expect some other?*' his reply was, '*Go and tell
John what you hear and see: the blind recover their sight, the lame walk . . .* '
(Matthew 11.3,4–5) This is why what happened that day in the House
of Mercy is a sign for the Jerusalem of Jesus' own day and for our world
also.

The next words in the Authorized Version, about the angel stirring up
the waters at certain times, are missing from all the earlier copies of the
Greek text and are relegated to a footnote in the Revised Version and
the NEB, so I think we can continue reading from verse 5.

Among them was a man who had been crippled for thirty-eight years. Now it
may be a coincidence, but according to Deuteronomy (chapter 2) 38
years was the duration of Israel's punitive wandering in the wilderness,
which may indicate that the Evangelist saw this incident as a type of a
whole people redeemed from impotence, from failure of nerve. *When
Jesus saw him lying there and was aware that he had been ill a long time, he
asked him, 'Do you want to recover?'* That was a devastatingly perceptive
question. For like so many people in deep depression the man believes
he is the victim of other people's indifference. '*Sir,' he replied, 'I have no
one to put me in the pool when the water is disturbed, but while I am moving,
someone else is in the pool before me.'*

12

That fits the picture revealed by the archaeologists: in that site there is a series of little shallow cisterns, each with room for only one person at a time. We should imagine that setting rather than a kind of swimming pool. *Jesus answered, 'Rise to your feet, take up your pallet bed and walk.'* By commanding the impossible – 'Stand up' – Jesus simply defied the man's inveterate, sulky dependence and released in him a new responsibility for his own life. *The man recovered instantly, took up his pallet, and began to walk.* ⋆

You must have noticed that, as often as not, Jesus insisted to an extraordinary degree on the co-operation of those he was healing, or those through whose trust the miracle was effected. The man with the withered arm must stretch it out. The man born blind must walk the length of the city, his eyes caked with clay, and wash it off. The ten with leprosy must simply take him at his word and report themselves to the priests as free of the disease; and only as they were going there did the healing take place. The palace officer from Capernaum, like the Syro-Phoenician mother, must turn round on the strength of his bare statement and go home to find the child recovered. The disciples must go and see how much food they can raise between themselves before the multitude can be fed. It isn't so much the crude wisdom of 'God helps them that help themselves' as the much stranger and much more profound truth that God chooses not to act solo in relation to the world, but always with and through its creatures. For it has been God's loving purpose from the beginning to raise those creatures to more and more responsible partnership with their Creator. That's the basis of all our thinking about partnership.

And now we meet the kind of religion that works against God by frustrating that purpose through making people dependent upon the guardians and the interpreters of a tradition (vv. 10-15⋆). *That day was a Sabbath. So the Jewish authorities said to the man who had been cured, 'It is the Sabbath. You are not allowed to carry your bed on the Sabbath.' He answered, 'The man who cured me said, "Take up your bed and walk."'* The one-time cripple had found a higher authority to appeal to than any prescribed custom. *They asked him, 'Who is the man who told you to take up your bed and walk?' But the cripple who had been cured did not know; for the place was crowded and Jesus had slipped away* – literally, 'had ducked aside'.

Jesus might evade the crowd, ducking aside, but he would never dodge the opportunity of carrying his contact with the man to a further level, a further degree of responsibility for the past and for the future. *A little later Jesus found him in the temple* (presumably giving thanks to God) *and said to him, 'Now that you are well again, leave your sinful ways,* (yes, sulky despair and passivity can be a besetting sin) *or you may suffer something worse'* – very stern advice, but loving. *The man went away and told the Jews that it was Jesus who had cured him* – not that it was Jesus who had made him carry his bed. The man was not transferring the blame this time, but giving credit where it belonged. It was Jesus who had cured him. That begged all their questions.

Now it is Jesus who has to face their questions (vv. 16–23). *It was works of this kind done on the Sabbath that stirred the Jews to persecute Jesus* – presumably through some official interrogation. They objected not so much to the acts themselves as to the principle that prompted Jesus to repeat them. It is this principle which he now puts into words. *He defended himself by saying, 'My Father has never yet ceased his work, and I am working too.'* Jesus went straight to the supposed origin of the Sabbath and the popular misunderstanding of it. They imagined a God who after six days of stupendous creative energy was withdrawn into a state of changeless stillness, of which the weekly Sabbath was meant to be a regular reminder. But Jesus contended that God's rest implies completion, not inaction. Had he not been for ever active on his people's behalf? 'My Father is at work up to this moment, and I am working too.'

If, according to the possibility I have mentioned, the festival for which he had come to Jerusalem was Yom Kippur, his answer was especially apposite, for according to very early Jewish tradition the Day of Atonement was the anniversary of the first day of creation, and an ancient prayer still used in the synagogue service for that day contains the words, 'This is the day of the beginning of thy works, a memorial of the first day when the remembrance of all that hath been formed cometh before thee.' And so Jesus says, 'My Father's unceasing work of maintaining the material universe in being, redeeming its mischances and its deviations, and restoring its life – all this has continued to this day, and so I work with him. I am his partner.' And in doing so Jesus is the fulfilment of God's age-long purpose, to raise up within created beings a responsible partner, a co-worker.

Hearing this, the inquisitors could only fasten upon the apparent blasphemy of the name 'Father'. *This made the Jews still more determined to kill him, because he was not only breaking the Sabbath,* literally 'untying' the Sabbath, *but, by calling God his own Father, he claimed equality with God.* They couldn't perceive, as St Paul was later able to do, that this Son did not think to snatch at equality with God, but sought only to be what all humanity was intended to be, God's responsive and responsible children and fellow workers. So to their charge of blasphemous presumption Jesus replied with what C. H. Dodd called The Parable of the Apprentice Son as a description of his own human relationship with God.

In very truth I tell you, the son (any apprentice son) *can do nothing by himself,* on his own; *he does only what he sees the father doing: whatever the father does, the son does. For the father loves the son and shows him all that he himself is doing, and will show him even greater deeds, to fill you with wonder.* ✶ The essence of all that this Father God is doing, and therefore of all that the human Son and partner does with him, is to bring a crippled, blind and impotent world to life. *As the Father is raising the dead and giving them life, so the Son gives life as he chooses,* ✶ (as he did at Bethesda that day). *Again, the Father does not judge anyone* – another central theme of the Day of Atonement – *but has given full jurisdiction to the Son,* the human partner, as he did when Jesus sought out the healed cripple in the temple. There he was coming as judge to warn him not to slip back into despair. And so God is bent upon making his human partner co-responsible.

It is his will, St John's Gospel goes on, *his purpose that all should pay the same honour to the Son as to the Father. To deny honour to the Son is to deny honour to the Father who sent him.*★ And that is speaking about the human son, the human partner. To deny honour to any of God's human partners is to deny honour to God. We mustn't be too quick to jump into the doctrine of the Trinity when we read St John. He is talking about sonship in its broadest meaning.

Of course Jesus was unique, I don't doubt that. He was the God-given archetype of creaturely response to God. Insofar as we can penetrate his mystery, I believe the Church was truly inspired to conclude that in him, in Jesus, God the Son, the eternal Son in the Trinity, was incarnate; which I take to mean that that in God which is eternally dedicated and obedient to God's own self-giving purpose became a man and lived out that divine obedience in the human response to God of Jesus of Nazareth, so bringing about that perfect partnership of the creature with the creator which was God's eternal purpose.

This uniqueness of Jesus, however, is sterile if it remains unique. He is, as the epistle to the Colossians puts it, *the beginning,* or as Paul wrote to the Romans, *the eldest among a large family of brothers and sisters,*★ or as the letter to the Hebrews says, *the pioneer* of God's design to bring many sons to glory (Colossians 1.18 RSV; Romans 8.29; Hebrews 2.10). And so we do not see a Jesus who hugs uniqueness to himself but rather one whose passion it was to share with others the relationship which he experienced towards God.

> . . . *no one knows the Father but the Son and those to whom the Son chooses to reveal him.*
> *So when you pray, say 'Abba'.*
> *You are the men who have stood firmly by me in my times of trial; and now I vest in you the kingship which my Father vested in me . . .*
>
> (Matthew 11.27; Luke 11.2★; 22.28-9)

Nor was it only that Jesus conferred on those who had faith in him the right to become children of God. He actually felt a profound need of their partnership, a human need of those men's company.

Twice over St Mark's Gospel brings this out, through its deliberate juxtaposition of events. Mark is an extraordinarily sophisticated

16

evangelist, and we need to see how it is that he has arranged the odd bits of the tradition which he had picked up and which he puts together in a specific order of his own designing.

In chapter 3 Jesus' choosing and empowering of the Twelve is followed and virtually explained by his natural family's faithlessness in accepting the innuendo of the Jerusalem scholars that he was possessed or out of his mind. Immediately after he'd gone up the mountain and called the Twelve, we are told that his own, his family, set out to take him in charge because they said, or they heard others say, 'He is possessed' (Mark 3.21). Next Mark exposes the origin of that calumny in the accusation of the scholars, and recounts how Jesus responded to it. And this leads at once to the scene in which the natural family of Jesus is 'outside', a word repeated three times over in this incident. And Jesus looks round the circle of his newly appointed companions, saying, '*Here are my mother and my brothers.*' (3.34) He needed a family that would believe in him.

The same poignant contrast is drawn in chapter 6 where Jesus' rejection by his home town, and his consequent impotence to heal people there, is immediately followed by the sending of the Twelve on their first mission with authority to preach and to heal. The home town rejects him so he must have his new family to go out and share his mission with him.

The partnership of Christ with his followers as partners together with God was to continue unbroken after the resurrection. In the earliest of his letters, the first to the Thessalonians, we find Paul describing Timothy as *our colleague and a fellow-worker with God in the service of the gospel of Christ.* Our colleague, another fellow worker with God. And later in his first epistle to the Corinthians he wrote, *After all, what is Apollos? What is Paul? Simply God's agents (diakonoi –* ministers, agents, deacons) *in bringing you to faith . . . We are God's fellow workers (sunergoi –* people who sweat and toil together, God's co-workers). And in a longer passage in 2 Corinthians, Paul develops the theme more dramatically, using the image of ambassadors or emissaries (*presbyteroi*):

> *God was in Christ reconciling the world to himself . . . and has*
> *entrusted us with the message of reconciliation. We are therefore*
> *Christ's ambassadors. It is as if God were appealing to you*
> *through us: we implore you in Christ's name, be reconciled to*
> *God! . . . Sharing in God's work, we make this appeal.*

(1 Thessalonians 3.2; 1 Corinthians 3.5,9; 2 Corinthians 5.19-6.1)

And there you have a superb description, it seems to me, of partnership, of mission partners. It involves the words 'deacons' and 'priests' for sure, but don't, for God's sake, let us limit it to those who are in the ordained ministry. For the final verses appended to St Mark's Gospel (16.20) also describe the mission of the young Church in terms of partnership: *they went out to proclaim their message far and wide, and the Lord worked with them . . .*

But this principle of the divine insistence upon a creaturely agent, perfectly actualized in Jesus Christ, wasn't at all new. It permeates the Jewish scriptures. These have been described as theology conveyed through narrative, of which the central actor is always God. Stories of God's action. That's a very helpful insight, and yet it needs to be said also that the stories invariably follow the career of a woman or a man whom God used – God's agents.

'*Shall I conceal from Abraham*', asks God, '*what I am about to do?*' A voice announces from the burning bush, '*I . . . have come down to rescue them . . . Come now; I will send you . . .*' That's the punchline, isn't it? 'I have come down to rescue you.' Wonderful; God is at last going to rescue his people. He's seen, he's heard, he's felt, he's going to come down. But he won't do it alone (Genesis 18.17; Exodus 3.7-10).

The psalmist says:

> *You guided your people like a flock*
> *shepherded by Moses and Aaron.*

The prophet Amos proclaims:

> *Indeed the Lord God does nothing without revealing his plan to*
> *his servants the prophets.*

(Psalm 77.20; Amos 3.7)

The divine insistence upon sharing responsibility with a human partner underlies the central idea of the Covenant. God's commitment to his people is a commitment to a mutual relationship. God surrenders unilateral sovereignty in order to involve them in responsibility for the future. Divine actions are not predetermined, for God is continually responding to the reactions of his people. That interaction all the time through history is God's partnership with wayward humanity. Quite apart from God's relation with humanity, however, this principle of the creaturely partner appears in the light of this century's physics and molecular chemistry to have characterized God's relation with the universe from the very start. Austin Farrer used the term 'Double Agency' to describe how God works upon the universe through the agency of its processes and the interplay of chance with inbuilt laws. He wrote, 'God made the world, but He did not just make it; He made it make itself'[1].

That insight of Austin Farrer is very apparent in the book of Genesis. We so often read that first chapter as though it was all God's act, or as I've suggested earlier, the action of the Holy Trinity upon the world; but it isn't. For no sooner have the sun and moon appeared than God gives them sovereignty, dominion, long before the dominion was given to humanity, to rule the whole movement of terrestrial time and to take over from God the separation of light and darkness. God turns to the earth and says, 'Bring forth.' God didn't just create fishes; somehow the water had to do it. God is constantly acting upon and using what is already there to go on to the next stage under his inspiration and in obedience to his word. That is a very Jewish insight, but it is absolutely fundamental for our understanding of Christ.

The same principle applies also to God's lordship over history. It isn't the Church only, nor the Chosen People alone, who serve God's long-laid purpose as his human partner. The Hebrew prophets recognized this, however shocking it was:

---

[1] *A Celebration of Faith: Selected Sermons by Austin Farrer*, Hodder & Stoughton, 1970, p. 73.

The Assyrian! He is the rod that I wield in my anger,
and the staff of my wrath is in his hand.
I send him against a godless nation,
I bid him march against a people who rouse my wrath . . .

I will send for my servant Nebuchadrezzar king of Babylon.
I will bring them against this land . . .

I am raising up the Chaldaeans,
that savage and impetuous nation,
who cross the wide tracts of the earth
to take possession of homes not theirs.

I say to Cyrus, 'You shall be my shepherd
to carry out all my purpose,
so that Jerusalem may be rebuilt
and the foundations of the temple may be laid.'

(Isaiah 10.5-6; Jeremiah 25.9; Habakkuk 1.6; Isaiah 44.28)

God isn't choosy. And if God chooses his human agents so indiscrim-
inately then who are we to refuse as fellow partners those who do or
don't ordain women, do or don't separate the orders of bishops and
presbyters?

And who cured Naaman? God, of course. But which human agent was
his partner in the curing of Naaman? The prophet Elisha? He sends
messages right and left, but he's never on the scene, which is rather
significant. That's what makes Naaman blow his top in fact. Let's look
at the story again (2 Kings 5). First there's a little Israelite maid who
has to say to her mistress. 'If only my master would go to Israel. There's
a prophet there who would make him well.' Then there must have
been some palace official who had overheard that child's remark and
went and told Naaman. Naaman himself goes and tells the King of
Syria. After that it begins to miss the point; it gets into the political
sphere. The King of Syria imagines he's got to send Naaman with a gift
on a proper diplomatic mission to the King of Israel. The King of Israel

reacts with panic because he thinks this is a plot. They are getting the whole thing hopelessly wrong, but nonetheless they are being used, they are part of a chain. Then someone with sense goes and tells Elisha. Elisha sends back somebody else with a message to the King of Israel. 'Send him to me, and he shall know that there is a prophet in Israel.' So at last Naaman arrives at Elisha's house. But he doesn't see Elisha. Yet another servant is sent out to give him the message. 'Go down to the Jordan and wash.' Naaman really gets angry then. And again it is his servants who turn the tables and say, 'This is a very simple thing to do, even if a bit humiliating, but there's nobody here from the press.' Nine different people, quite apart from Elisha, have to play their part. However uncomprehending, however small, they are all God's partners. God is using them.

Yet it is still to Jesus Christ that we must look if we are to grasp the essential nature and pattern of the partnership that God looks for and intends for humanity, for he alone has perfectly mirrored in a human life the eternal co-operation of the Father and the Son within the triune God. That pattern, which all who would be consciously God's fellow workers must aspire to, became clear to Jesus at his baptism, we are told, by the conjunction of two Old Testament images. 'Thou art my beloved son', echoing Psalm 2 and other passages, evokes the figure of the Messiah-King. 'In whom I am well pleased,' or 'On whom my favour rests,' is a phrase drawn from a very different image, the servant who must suffer. As far as I know, the two figures had never been brought together in the Jewish consciousness up to that moment. The servant in suffering, the Messiah who must go down rather than up, the self-given Son, *he* is God's partner. And to be called into part-nership with him is to be called into his sonship. *To those who have yielded him their allegiance he gave the right to become children of God –* self-given, like him (John 1.12). We must honour all who share that vocation, those we know, whoever they may be, and those we don't know.

3

God's temple

Our recognition of God's habitual insistence upon working in partnership with a creaturely agent compels us to see the world, its life and
its history, as the arena of God's action and ours. We turn now to the
biblical image of the temple for the light it throws on our understanding of the Church and its place in God's purpose. The insights of
St John's Gospel are particularly significant as they emerge in chapters
2 and 4.

The wedding at Cana (2.1-11) may not seem very relevant to the
temple theme. Weddings, after all, belong to the common experience of
all humanity; they are celebrations of the vitality and hope of the whole
world – and, incidentally, one of the Church's most natural and valuable
points of contact with the life of the world. But this story does contain
one very pertinent implication for our understanding of the Church and
the gospel, one which is, I believe, the crux of the narrative.

I want to suggest that the writer of this fourth Gospel kept in mind
the outline pattern of Mark's Gospel even while he set about redress-
ing its omission of Christ's Judaean ministry, which was his main
interest. So, after the prelude, he starts, like Mark, with John the Baptist,
and follows up with the call, first of leading apostles, and then of lesser
known disciples. In Mark's pattern this leads to the beginning of
tension between the message of Jesus and the Jewish traditions,
culminating in the feast in Levi's house and the various sayings about
new wine and new cloth. So it seems to me that this is also the inner
significance to which the Evangelist is pointing in this 'beginning of
signs', as he calls it. The incident follows upon an initial inadequacy –
the wine gave out. There are moments in history when that happens to
a whole culture, a whole religious tradition. It was true of Judaism in
the first century AD, especially in Judaea under the Sadducee high

priesthood; in many ways it is true of European Christianity now. There is an ancient Jewish saying: 'Without wine there is no joy.' Moreover it looks as if it was actually the unexpected arrival of Jesus that precipitated the crisis. *The mother of Jesus was there*, it says - one of the invited guests, presumably as a friend of the family, since Cana lies only four and a half miles from Nazareth. Then it adds: *Jesus also was invited and his disciples**★** - not 'had been invited', but *eklethe*, was invited then and there. Six young men turned up as the party was starting, and Eastern hospitality demanded that they be made welcome. No wonder the wine gave out! Yet Eastern hospitality also demanded that lavish extra provision be made for emergencies. Unpreparedness had been found out, as in so many of the parables of Jesus.

Next comes the note of divergence between Jesus and his mother. *Jesus's mother said to him, 'They have no wine left.'* Maybe she held him responsible and thought he should do something about it. Perhaps, as his response appears to suggest, she saw this as the moment for launching a public ministry in the north. Whatever was in her mind, it did not accord with his own sense of direction. 'Let me alone, lady,' is the gist of his answer. It is a common, almost untranslatable query in Hebrew: 'What is there to me and to you?' The widow of Zarapheth says it to her lodger, Elijah, when her young son dies: 'Leave me alone! Why did you ever interfere?' (1 Kings 17.18) David says it to the loyal courtier who offers to knock off the head of the man who is showering him with curses: 'Your ideas are not mine' (2 Samuel 16.10). The Pharaoh Necho, leading his army against Assyria, says it to Josiah King of Judah who insists upon crossing swords with him at Megiddo. 'Mind your own business. I've no quarrel with you' (2 Chronicles 35.21). So this was the tenor of Jesus' reply to his mother. 'Leave me alone, dear mother. It isn't time yet for a Galilean ministry.' But the point that the Evangelist has established through their exchange of words is that of divergence. Here is a late arrival who has his own ideas: 'My thoughts are not your thoughts.'

Jesus' next action is clearly symbolic. *There were six stone water-jars . . . each held from twenty to thirty gallons.* The Evangelist is at pains to point out that these had a ritual function: they provided for the *washing of cups and jugs and copper bowls* mentioned in Mark's Gospel (7.4), and for the ablution of hands and head before meals enjoined by the laws of religion which were to be a bone of contention between Jesus and the authorities early in his ministry. The six water jars represented the old regime, the tradition, and at the bidding of Jesus the household servants filled them up to the brim. *'Do not suppose that I have come to abolish the Law and the prophets; I did not come to abolish, but to complete,'* to fulfil (Matthew 5.17). So out to the well go the servants, and back and forth until the stone jars are brim full.

But how do you bring an old and precious spiritual heritage to its fullness and completeness? Is that done by perpetuating and conserving? *Jesus said to the servants . . . 'Antlēsate nun,* now draw water *and take it to the steward of the feast'.* There are no grounds for translating the words as 'Now draw some off' or implying that it came from the water jars. The verb *antleo* is used in the New Testament and in the Septuagint translation of the Old Testament only of drawing water from a well, and the noun formed from it, *antlēma,* means a bucket, not a jug. *'Antlēsate nun'*, said Jesus. 'Go back to the well again, to the source from which the water pots of the tradition were supplied, and draw from that original source what is needed *now.* Don't take it second hand, stored and passed on, but go yourself to the fountain head, serve it new for today, and it will be wine, and the best wine at that.'

So then, after a brief interval at Capernaum with his family and the few new disciples, Jesus returned to Judaea to keep the Passover at Jerusalem; there we take up the story (2.12-21).

This Gospel brings out the fact that before launching his own style of mission in Galilee, Jesus did work closely with John the Baptist for a period. During that time it looked as if he had accepted the role of the Coming One as John visualized it, as the agent of judgement and purification, even to the point of acting out the part of the Messenger, foretold by Malachi, who should suddenly come to God's Temple with refining fire. Be that as it may, the Gospel reports that it was at this early stage in his short public career that Jesus found in the very precincts of the temple *the dealers in cattle, sheep, and pigeons, and the money-changers seated at their tables.* Jesus had good reason to be appalled and affronted, not so much by the presence of traders doing business in the outer court as by the racketeering it represented. Annas, who had become High Priest when Jesus was about twelve, established his dynasty so firmly that five of his sons, a son-in-law and a grandson all succeeded him in the office at different times. They drew more or less any salary they chose from the Temple treasury and owned a virtual monopoly of all the trade in animals required for sacrifice – many thousands of them every year. So they were immensely rich and universally hated. The action of Jesus on this occasion was a bold public protest which they can never have forgiven. His disciples, this Gospel tells us, recalled (no doubt with a justifiable foreboding) the words of Scripture, *Zeal for thy house will destroy me.*

But the Evangelist wants to make more than a historical point out of the incident. He sees it as calling in question the traditional under-standing of worship as such, and of the nature of the religious community, the Church. So he goes on:

> The Jews challenged Jesus: 'What sign', they asked, 'can you show as authority for your action?' 'Destroy this temple,' Jesus replied, 'and in three days I will raise it again.' They said, 'It has taken forty-six years to build this temple. Are you going to raise it again in three days?' But the temple he was speaking of was his body. After his resurrection his disciples recalled what he had said, and they believed the Scripture and the words that Jesus had spoken.

'*Destroy this temple*' – 'bring it to dissolution' is the force of the word, 'undo it totally' – '*and in three days I will raise it up.*' The Gospel of John is the only one which claims that Jesus did actually use these much dis-puted words. Mark and Matthew tell us that this was the one charge on which the corrupt witnesses against him did more or less agree. Luke, writing in the Acts of the Apostles, says that the charge against Stephen was that he had been heard to say that 'Jesus of Nazareth will destroy this place.' We are clearly dealing with a very strong tradition that Jesus had certainly predicted, if not actually threatened, the destruction of the temple, a tradition which the authorities interpreted in one way and the followers of Jesus in another. The words in which the saying was recalled in the Christian community, with the mention of three days and the use of that verb *egeiro*, raise up, shows that they very soon associated them with the resurrection, even though they may not have admitted that Jesus spoke them. On the other hand the high-priestly clique had been left in no doubt about Jesus' hostility towards their regime. His demonstration in the Temple had made that abundantly clear, and others of his sayings may have been reported to them: 'Have you not read that . . . *the priests in the temple break the Sabbath and it is not held against them? I tell you, there is something greater than the temple here.*' (Matthew 12.5-6) So Annas and his son-in-law, Joseph Caiaphas, could well have believed that Jesus had threatened the dissolution of the Temple. And that need not mean that they took his words literally, even if they allowed others in the Sanhedrin to do so. To say that Jesus was condemned on a misunderstanding is over-simplifying the facts and making Caiaphas and his circle a lot more stupid than they were. He was a subtle enemy, well versed in allegory, who probably understood Jesus better than many of the disciples. He could quite well grasp Jesus' meaning and recognize that he was in fact set upon building a new temple that would supercede the old. That was indeed why he had to be killed. The taunts that the priests hurled at Jesus on Golgotha (Matthew 27.40) reveal a definite inkling that this body, now safely crucified, might have become an alternative to their Temple, though the possibility of its resurrection never crossed their minds. '*You would pull the temple down, would you, and build it in three days? Come down from the cross and save yourself . . .*'

What is the significance of a temple and what is its place in the purposes of God? About a thousand years before Jesus challenged the hierarchy Solomon had built the first Temple on the same site to the north of the city of David. It towered above the narrow streets with the palace beside it. As in many a mediaeval city, the two buildings might seem to represent dominance in a divided society, but could also be seen to symbolize the community as a people with a single name under law and under God, evidence of a divine purpose being fulfilled in history. In his prayer at the dedication of the Temple Solomon may have caught a hazy glimpse of that purpose when he asked, '*Can God indeed dwell on earth?*' (1 Kings 8.27) But Solomon was thinking primarily of himself and of God's guarantee to David that his dynasty would retain the throne. He could not see, and probably did not care, that the monarchy, the temple and the city itself, all promised by God, were only symbols of the fulfilment of God's supreme purpose and desire, the creation of a human community responsive to the divine love.

Shrines and sanctuaries have meant so much to the human spirit, and still have power to bestow a unifying sense of transcendence as nothing else can. But precisely because of the mysterious influence of places, shrines and sanctuaries have often exacted a fearful toll of human lives and mental freedom. They have been points of bitter contention as often as a focus of unity. This is the theme which the Fourth Gospel picks up in the conversation by the well in chapter 4, verses 19–26. '*Our fathers worshipped on this mountain, but you Jews say that the temple where God should be worshipped is in Jerusalem.*' This was not a merely theological dispute; blood had been shed and the Jerusalem Temple desecrated. '*Believe me,*' said Jesus, '*the time is coming when you will worship the Father neither on this mountain, nor in Jerusalem.*' This does not imply that there are no degrees of truth or that all beliefs are of equal value. '*You Samaritans worship without knowing what you worship, while we worship what we know. It is from the Jews that salvation comes*' – yet only inasmuch as it is living water drawn afresh from the well; only when it is a corporately lived experience, not a tradition of beliefs and observances dispensed from ancient storage jars. Jesus, while living out his own life of perfect human response and partnership with God, looked to a future when the same response and partnership will find more general embodiment, not in a shrine but in a community. '*The time is coming, indeed it is already here, when true worshippers will worship the Father,* the God whom we know as Father, *in spirit and in truth,* in their spirit and their reality. *These are the worshippers the Father wants.*' The new temple is not a holy place, but a holy people.

In the Samaritan woman's book that kind of religion won't be much in evidence until Messiah comes. '*I am he, I who am speaking to you now.*' Here was the answer to the question Solomon had asked rhetorically when dedicating his Jerusalem Temple: 'Can God really live with humanity here on earth?' Yes, the Word became flesh and tabernacled among us. Here is God's temple, God's *shekinah* glory, God's presence in a living man wholly responsive, wholly responsible, crucified, dead, buried, raised again and at large in the world forever. '*The temple he was speaking of was his body.*'

'Thou, O God, art in the midst of us and we are called by thy name.' The familiar reading from the ancient office of Compline affirms our Christian experience of the presence of the incarnate God: in the midst of all humanity in the temple of the body of Jesus of Nazareth suffering and dying; in the midst of all humanity in the temple of that man's body risen and glorified; in the midst of all humanity in the temple of that man's body which is now the body of all who have been baptized in faith into his death and resurrection. For thereby, if they will but accept it, they become in their shared life and action the on-going physical being of that one man, which alone is God's true temple in the midst of the world.

You are God's building, wrote Saint Paul to the Corinthians; and again, *Surely you know that you are God's temple where the Spirit of God dwells.* (1 Corinthians 3.9,16) He was careful to say that about them in the plural, but we, like Solomon at the dedication of his Temple, are quick to apply the attribution to ourselves as individuals. This is understand-able because our experiences of direct encounter with God occur almost always when we are on our own. Yet those experiences, by their very nature, can never be put into adequate words, though they may change the rest of a life. So it is not true, as the saying has it, that religion is what people do with their solitude. Religion is very much more how people relate to each other and to God in the light of certain corporately remembered solitary experiences - their own or, more often, other people's in the past. We are not meant to think of our individual selves as local shrines of the Holy Spirit. In Old Testament times local shrines fostered idiosyncracy and idolatry, and they do so still. It was a great step forward for Judaism when King Josiah abolished them and centralized the nation's worship in the one Temple in Jerusalem. St Paul too knew that there is only one true temple of God in our midst, so he addressed his fellow Christians corporately in the plural: 'You as a community are God's temple.' He understood, as did the writer of the Fourth Gospel, that 'the temple he was speaking of was Christ's body'.

Call this talk of incorporation into Christ's body, if you wish, a mythical way of saying that the fulfilment of God's eternal purpose, having been accomplished in that one human life of perfect response and sonship, is now being expanded and extended as the followers of that Son of God are empowered by his Spirit to embody the same response of sonship in their love of one another and their corporate action in the world. Myth or metaphor it may be, but what it expresses is no less real. It is, indeed, a fact of common experience that any close-knit association, sharing the idea of a charismatic founder and living it out as a family, has a unique power, for better or worse, to draw, inspire and sustain new followers. As God the Son took a natural human body for his incarnation, so has he used a natural human phenomenon to create his mystical body as the extension of that incarnation. In the happy acceptance of one another by people who have little in common except Christ, in their readiness to talk honestly and work selflessly together because they are Christ's - rich and poor, high-brow and low-brow, black, brown and white, lay and ordained, Catholic and Protestant, convinced and questioning - this is where God's temple, which is Christ's body, stands, drawing all nations into God's embrace.

Only by constantly recalling that its true identity is Christ alone can the Church escape from being just another religious institution. In her *form* that is, of course, exactly what she is - a creed, a cult and a code of behaviour, with pundits, priests and prelates to manage them. It is the form that every religious institution takes as the best means of conserving an original inspiration and handing it on. But that necessary function and form compel the Church to become just another of the storage jars. Only by being Christ himself can the Christian community remain the source of that living water which is also the wine of life. It is Christ in his body the Church, and no-one else, who absolves and blesses, baptizes and marries and ordains; and in the Eucharist consecrates and offers his very self to the Father as his unceasing human response of sonship and partnership. This is why the celebrant, as an authorized representative of the whole Church, is required to use the plural 'we' throughout the eucharistic prayer, so that any obtrusion of the first person singular jars on the ear.

So we are brought back to the eternal purpose of the Father that Christ's perfect offering of human response should be made, first *on behalf of*, but ultimately *inclusive of* all humanity and all creation. The body of Christ, growing from the living nucleus of Jesus of Nazareth, is to culminate, not as a section of humanity called the Church, but as a total humanity gathered and incorporated into his life of perfect response to God and responsibility for the world. Our togetherness as Christians remains an ineffectual sentiment until we discover one another's indispensable value as colleagues in service to the world, a service that may sometimes take the form of challenging and destroying old temples and taking the consequence, as Jesus did.

Yes, we have to come to that sooner or later, since that is what a temple is for: a place of sacrifice. If we are the body of Christ it is for death and resurrection. Because we are Christ's body we are the martyr church, committed to a ceaseless giving away of life for truth and in love. 'We are the Body . . . This is my Body . . .' The two statements go together inseparably to their completion. That is the only possible pattern of the self-giving God's presence within his creation, the temple not made with hands.

4

God's time

Christopher Dawson's great book on the making of Europe[1] shows that the year 1000 was indeed a watershed between the Dark Ages and the dawn of a new civilization. But the imminent approach of that millennium caused widespread anxiety and many crazy reactions. It looks as if a second millennium may have the same effect. Overmuch obsession with time seems always to raise the level of human insecurity. It happens when we hear time's 'wingèd chariot drawing near', or when the overwhelming durations of astronomy bring home our insignificance. A millennium or a centenary may be a good moment for taking stock, but may induce us to make very wrong decisions if the way we visualize time is at fault.

There are actually three ways in which it is possible to picture the flow of events, according to the point from which we think of that stream of events emerging. Where does it come from? Do you think of this morning as something which has come to you out of the past with its circumstances shaped and determined by past decisions and events? Obviously it *has* come from the past in one sense. Or are you able to imagine a new day which has flowed towards you out of the future so that it has come into your hands unknown, as a gift waiting to be unwrapped, part of the purpose intended for you? Or do you see today in all its given circumstances good and bad as the only real starting point, the first day of the rest of your life? Do you recognize instinctively that now is the only moment in which you and everything else can actually exist? *Behold, now is the proper, the favourable, time, now the day of deliverance.* (2 Corinthians 6.2★)

---

[1] *The Making of Europe – 400-1000 AD*, Sheed and Ward, 1932.

In our Western culture most people see the present as determined by the past because science has won its achievements by looking always for the antecedent causes of things, asking what conditions or what change has brought this about. It's actually very hard for us to allow for any other kind of cause. And this, applied to our personal lives, burdens us with those doom-laden questions, 'What did I do wrong?' 'If only my parents had . . .' and so on. It comes as a surprise to realize that the biblical concept of time, in fact the whole pre-scientific idea of causation that persisted right through the Middle Ages, tended much more towards the second way of thinking, which sees the present coming out of the future. In this view things are explained by the purpose for which they exist. Plants produce leaves, said Aristotle, to protect the fruit when it appears. The Old Testament assumes that the history of Israel unfolded as it did because of the final purpose God had in view, to create a holy people as an example for all humanity.

In the New Testament the resurrection of Jesus and the resurrection life of the Christian had no antecedent cause. And that's what makes it so difficult for our scientific age to believe in it. It has no antecedent cause. It comes as a gift from the future. The counterpart of this joyful expectancy, however, is an apocalyptic dread, *men fainting with fear and with foreboding of what is coming on the world,* doomed to *a fearful prospect of judgement.* (Luke 21.26 RSV; Hebrews 10.27 RSV) So both the antecedent and the teleological (as it's called) view of causation can too easily turn into fatalism.

Either that or, just as fatally, they may turn into fantasy. Many people and many nations are haunted by a past that never was; distorted memories, good or bad, have become part of their culture. On the other hand eschatology, God's genuine promise, may too easily become human fantasy when we pretend to know more than has been promised. Then we live with backward-looking eschatology, that contradiction in terms that is plaguing the land of Israel today. When we try to see too far ahead we always get it wrong. '*It is not for you to know times past or seasons yet to come, which the Father has firmly in his own hands. But you are to receive power when the Holy Spirit comes upon you and you shall be my witnesses . . .*' (Acts 1.7-8*) That is enough for now. And now is what matters, for only the third way of looking at time, which was Jesus' way, can save us from becoming the anxious puppets either of history or destiny, and set us free to be responsible under God for our own lives and the life of his world.

I think this concept of time is very important for us whose job it is to plan, and who now are anxiously planning not just for a centenary in the case of some of us, but for a millennium.

Christians have sometimes created an unreal burden for themselves out of the obligation to discern the signs of the times, imagining that the phrase implies a degree of prophecy beyond that of ordinary perception. But the phrase in the Gospels actually refers to an ability to see the implication of events that are taking place in the present, and that requires simple honesty and lack of prejudice rather than any special gift of clairvoyance. And so Jesus condemned the Phariseees and Sadducees for their deliberate blindness in refusing to recognize the signs, the obvious significance of his miracles of deliverance. '*If I in the spirit of God am now casting out demons, then has the Kingdom of God* (God's rule) *already come upon you*'. (Matthew 12.28)

But discerning the signs of the times also refers to the forseeable outcome of present policies and attitudes. Jesus, like Isaiah and Jeremiah before him, was clear-sighted enough – but not clairvoyant – clear-sighted enough to see that his nation's proud and worldly interpretation of their vocation as the People of God, and their rejection of his own understanding of the Kingdom of God, must lead inexorably to a fatal conflict with Rome with all its predictable horrors. He could see that well enough. He could see the choice being made in a wrong direction, but they were blind to it.

> '*When you see clouds gathering in the west, you say at once, "It is going to rain," and rain it does. And when the wind is from the south, you say, "It will be hot," and it is. What hypocrites you are! You know how to interpret the appearance of earth and sky, but cannot interpret this fateful hour.*'

> '*If only you had known this day the way that leads to peace! But no; it is hidden from your sight. For a time will come upon*

> *you, when your enemies will set up siege-works against you . . .
> and not leave you one stone standing on another, because you
> did not recognize the time of God's visitation.'*

(Luke 12.54-6; 19.42-4)

That word 'visitation' may imply God's coming either for redemption
or judgement or both at once. But the point is that what has to be
discerned and acted upon is now, observable *in this your day*, in this
moment of time. Jesus doesn't call us to guess the future, but to respond
rightly to the present, and that will determine what the future brings.

Jesus' way of looking at time is demonstrated very clearly in the story
of the raising of Lazarus and it is a rewarding exercise to look at the
passage in detail (John 10.40 – 11.44).

*Jesus withdrew again across the Jordan, to the place where John had been
baptizing.* There had been several such withdrawals during his ministry.
After the show-down of his demonstration in the Temple and the
arrest of John the Baptist at the beginning, he had gone away from
Judaea to start his quite different Galilean ministry. And then following the feeding of the multitude, when the crowd tried to make a rebel
leader of him, he had withdrawn beyond the jurisdiction of Herod
Antipas into Phoenicia and Ituria. It was now the winter before his
arrest and crucifixion, only a few more months yet. And during
Hanukkah, the Festival of Lights, he had narrowly missed a summary
execution by stoning similar to Stephen's a year or so later. Hence this
withdrawal out of Judaea over the Jordan into what we now call the
Kingdom of Jordan, to a spot where his ministry with the Baptist had
first begun and, according to verse 41, was still remembered.

There was to be one further brief withdrawal from the capital following
the Sanhedrin's formal decision to proceed against him, but by then the
die was already cast and he knew it. The Gospels present us with a man
pursuing a steadfast path who nonetheless took his cue from events and
responded to them, as an opportunist almost, moment by moment. Now
the prepositions in verse 1 of chapter 11 are interesting because they
link this family with the Martha and Mary of St Luke's Gospel. I give
a translation that brings out these prepositions.

Now there was a man of Bethany named Lazarus who was ill,
a native of the village of Martha and her sister Mary [that vil-
lage where Jesus had stopped with them further north]. *That was the Mary who anointed the Lord with ointment and*
wiped his feet with her hair, whose brother Lazarus had fallen
ill. The sisters therefore sent a message to him, 'Sir, you should
know that your friend lies ill.'

Those words don't necessarily imply a call for help. As Lazarus grew
worse the sisters must often have murmured, 'If only Jesus was here.'
But they wouldn't have wanted to bring him back into the peril that
he had only recently escaped, which they certainly knew about. They
agreed eventually that at least they should let him know. After all he
had healed some folk without going in person to their homes.

But in fact they were too late. For Jesus was a two days' journey away,
and so, according to the times given by the Evangelist, by the time the
message had been delivered to him Lazarus was already dead. It may
be that, through his extraordinary empathy with people, Jesus knew
that or came to realize it soon after. And yet his immediate response to
the message was supremely positive and life-affirming. '*This sickness is*
not unto death (AV), not tending towards death, it shall not serve death's
purpose.' It is an interesting construction in the Greek. It is the same
in Acts 27.12, *The harbour being unsuitable (pros paracheimasian) to serve*
the purpose of wintering.⋆ And in Ephesians 4.12 where Paul speaks of
the Lord's provision of apostles, prophets, pastors, evangelists and so on
(*pros ton katartismon*) *to promote the upbuilding of the saints.*⋆ Or in 1
Timothy 4.7, where Timothy is encouraged to train like an athlete
(*pros eusebeian*) *to advance your devotion in the Lord.*⋆ And so, says Jesus,
'*This sickness is not death's lackey, but it is for the glory of God, that the Son*
of God may be glorified.'

What are we to make of that? On the face of it it strikes me as an
appalling remark. Is a friend to succumb to a fatal sickness and his
family suffer days of anxiety and then mourning, in order that Jesus can
work a supreme miracle and win credit for God? That's what the words
seem to mean to our modern ears. Can we respect a Creator who fixes
things at our expense for his own glorification? What I find even more

shocking than that thought is the fact that, when something in the Bible outrages us like this, the conventional response is to suppress our spontaneous rejection and look for some dutiful justification for such a God. I want to say as strongly as I can that if the Bible is to be God's word to us and guide us into truth, then we ourselves must be true in our conversation with it and not try to be polite or conceal our reactions to it. And so, for example, when we meet this difficult saying of Jesus, a much more honest reaction should be, 'Jesus can't possibly have said what this seems to mean. Therefore I haven't understood what it really does mean. We must look at it again.'

'This sickness is not unto death, but for the sake of the glory of God, that by its means the Son of God may be glorified.' Perhaps this time you notice that what Jesus said contains no reference whatever to the cause of his friend's sickness, nor any suggestion that God was responsible or allowed it to happen; only that it *would* serve God's purpose, God's glory. And to glorify means to let the true nature, the inner nature shine out. Self-aggrandizement at the expense of others is not the true nature of God or of Jesus. Jesus in fact never asked what caused a misfortune or why it was sent. For him the only question that mattered was, 'Now, what shall we make of this?' It's happened; what purpose shall it serve? On this occasion what his words mean is, 'This sickness shall not serve death's purpose, but it shall be the means whereby the true nature of God and of his servant-Son will shine out.'

What Jesus understood by the true nature of God and how it was to shine out in him remains to be seen. But he knew. He had made his decision without any hesitation: the outcome was to be a victory for life, not for death. He had made that decision out of love, out of a very great love. For it is exactly at this point, immediately after that declaration of intention, that the Gospel inserts the statement, *Now Jesus loved Martha and her sister and Lazarus.* (RSV) Because of love the outcome was going to be life, not death. Yet he waited two days. Knowing intuitively that his friend had died, there was no need to rush back. But having resolved what to make of the tragedy, why did Jesus hold back? What was he doing for those two days? His next words to the disciples give us the clue. *'Let us go back to Judaea.'* It was Judaea that had been on his mind during that mysterious two-day hesitation, not

36

Bethany, not Lazarus and the sisters. It was going to be life for them; but the price of that life – Judaea. The disciples knew at once what that name meant. *'Master, it was only just now that the Jews tried to stone you. Are you going there again?'*★

His reply is enigmatic. 'There are only twelve hours of daylight, aren't there? The time for travelling is then, when you can see the road. If you leave it too late when it is dark again, you will stumble.' So, I wonder, had Jesus experienced that nightfall, that loss of direction during the two days while he wrestled with the implications of his decision? It is one thing to decide to cross the Rubicon. It is another to start visualizing the dreaded battle which must follow. And everything in this story suggests that in the eyes of the fourth Evangelist this was Jesus' Gethsemane. When he comes to the real Gethsemane it is nothing but calm, nothing but self-possession, nothing but thought for others. The Evangelist seems to place the agony that the other Gospels describe in the Garden in these two days, and also in his approach to the tomb before raising Lazarus from death. So after the darkness and the awful wrestling of indecision, or at least of dread, has he determined to seize a new moment of clarity to make the fatal journey without any further stumbling in the dark of temptation?

Then Jesus explains what it was that had prompted his decision, first of all in metaphor, *'Our friend Lazarus has fallen asleep, but I shall go and wake him,'* and then with brutal directness, *'Lazarus is dead.'* And at that the thought returns to Jesus, 'What are we going to make of this?', followed by a renewal of joy. *'I am glad for your sake that I was not there* (to prevent this death), *for it will lead you to believe.'* To believe in what? To believe, to trust in the true nature of God.

So on the third day after receiving the message from Bethany they started the arduous journey back. A good twelve miles down to the Jordan Valley and then across it, hot even in the early weeks of the year, followed by a steep climb of over three thousand feet in seventeen miles. The village street of Bethany on the edge of the Jerusalem escarpment commands a long view of the road winding up from the valley. The approaching travellers could have been seen a long way off by any of those friends who had come out from the city two miles away to condole with Martha and Mary. No doubt it was from some of them that Jesus learned that Lazarus had been entombed four days before, while others passed the word on to Martha, 'Jesus is coming.'

Without disturbing her distraught sister she hurries out to meet him and comes upon his party just beyond the end of the village. See them there, those two face to face in the late afternoon sun, the woman whose practical strength had carried the main burden of her brother's illness and death and burial, and the exhausted traveller who is the family's special friend.

> *'Lord, if you had been here my brother would not have died. Even now I know that God will grant you whatever you ask of him.'*
>
> *'Your brother will rise again.'*
>
> *'I know that he will rise again, at the resurrection . . . on the last day.'*
>
> *'I am the resurrection and the life. Whoever has faith in me shall live, even though he dies; and no one who lives and has faith in me shall ever die. Do you believe this?'*
>
> *'I do, Lord . . . I believe that you are the Messiah, the Son of God who was to come into the world.'*

For me this is possibly the most intense and dramatic conversation in the Bible. It is pure drama because so much is being said, so many cross-purposes concealed, in so few words. How is it that, as we read it, we feel so much is going on between Jesus and Martha? And how is it that we too are so involved in what is going on?

Look at the details, look at the tenses. They are always important in the Bible. The conversation starts with Martha's spontaneous cry, 'Lord, if you had been here . . .' It wasn't necessarily complaint or recrimination. They accepted the fact that he couldn't be there. And yet, if only. And now, when, against all hope, she sees him there, but too late, her imagination turns back the clock. 'Oh, if only, how different it could have been.' In moments of stress people so often reconstruct the past. Haven't you? Do you recognize a habitual tendency of your own in Martha's cry? Can you remember the last time you said, 'If we hadn't done such and such this wouldn't have happened' or, 'I ought to have done so and so instead'? I suppose it releases the anxiety a bit if you can blame it on some mistaken moment in the past. How much anger does it express, I wonder? And what kind of a map of human destiny do we create by a habitual use of this backward-looking 'if only'? Am I really trailing behind myself a history of mistakes? And is that a view of life which I am meant to have?

As if consciously correcting a tendency in herself, Martha immediately adds the words, '*Even now I know that God will grant you whatever you ask of him.*' That sounds a bit more positive, but what did Martha have in mind? Did she even know what she meant? Or was it just a way of saying, 'Over to you'? So often people in distress make these conventional statements of belief, but if you listen to them, there's not much in them. They are grasping at straws. Jesus' reply is strangely brief and matter-of-fact. '*Your brother will rise again.*' No question about it. Martha interprets it in the only sense she knows, the only sense in which her church, or our church for that matter, seems able to understand it.

'*I know that he will rise again at the resurrection on the last day.*' Have you noticed the tense she has been using? Ever since that first habitual, backward-looking, 'If only', Martha has swung into the future tense. 'I know God will grant you whatever you ask of him.' 'I know my brother will rise again on the last day.' And in both cases her future expectations sound as vague and platitudinous as all such comforting daydreams. 'God will answer our prayers.' 'We'll meet again in God's good time.' Can you recall when you last grasped at the future to help you get through the present?

But Jesus cuts right across Martha's obsessions with a might-have-been past and a never-never future. When he said, 'Your brother will rise again,' he was talking about now. And it could only make sense in the light of what he said next, 'I am.' That was the present reality. It still is.

> '*If you had been here my brother would not have died.*'
> '*I am here.*'
> '*I know he will rise again at the resurrection on the last day.*'
> '*I am the resurrection. I am life.*'*

39

It is all now. The present is where we start from. It was the same with that other woman.

> *'I know that when Messiah comes he will explain everything.'*
> *'I, talking with you now, am He.'*
>
> (John 4.25-6*)

Or the dying thief:

> *'Remember me when you come into your Kingdom.'*
> *'Today, with me.'*
>
> (Luke 23.42,43*)

For those who have faith in Jesus Christ the present is the only tense. They can call in that part of themselves that dwells in the past with its regrets and resentments and scars. They can call in that part of themselves that lives in the future amid fears, ambitions and daydreams. Yes, of course, past and future do affect us, but they affect us today. They are factors of our present. And with us now and only now is the Living One - Life itself giving itself as he did for Lazarus, his friend.

And how *does* life give itself? By means of that mysterious law of the universe which Charles Williams called the Doctrine of Exchange. We can and do bear one another's burdens. One can lift away another person's fear or anxiety by undertaking to become worried or terrified instead. We've almost lost the use of such powers, but they exist, and I think that most mothers are aware of them, and some lovers too. The capacity exists because it is the Creator's own reflection within his creation. Life lives by giving itself away out of love. It gives life to the dead by undergoing their death. That is the glory, the true nature of God. That is what is going to shine out now, and Jesus knew that the hour had come for that sacrificial nature to shine out. By coming to give life to Lazarus, and not only Lazarus but to God's whole beloved humanity, he had handed himself over to his destroyers.

It was the other sister Mary who witnessed and to some degree shared his Gethsemane. She in her turn comes running and throws herself at his feet, sobbing, '*If you had only been here.*' And her anguish seems to have triggered off his own. The language which St John's Gospel uses has baffled most commentators, for it describes not the confident approach to an act of triumphant power, but a terrible inner conflict. The words of the narrative literally mean: *He was swept by agitation of spirit and shuddering distress . . . He shuddered inwardly.* (John 11.33, 38*) That portrayal is reminiscent of St Mark's description of the agony in the garden (Mark 14.33-4): *Horror and anguish overwhelmed him, and he said to them, 'My heart is ready to break with grief . . .'* Then, as in Gethsemane, he went forward. *'Take away the stone.'* The great cry, *'Lazarus, come out!'* And then the final practical command, *'Loose him; let him go'* – the very phrase he was to use in Gethsemane again (John 18.8): *'If I am the man you want, let these others go.'*

As if to underline the price that Jesus paid for restoring life to Lazarus and hope to that family, St John's Gospel rounds off the story with an ominous epilogue (John 11.45-53): *Some of them went off to the Pharisees and reported what he had done. Thereupon the chief priests and the Pharisees convened a meeting of the Council . . . One of them, Caiaphas, who was High Priest that year, said . . . 'It is more to your interest that one man should die for the people, than that the whole nation should be destroyed.'*

We do not have the power to raise the dead. We haven't got such supreme aliveness in ourselves for that. Yet Jesus calls us to obey the inner law of life. Life exists by giving itself away. *'Whoever gains his life will lose it; whoever loses his life for my sake will gain it.'* (Matthew 10.39)

It seems certain that the next few decades will bring more rapid and more far-reaching change to the whole world than anyone can remember or visualize. Yet Christ's mandate to his followers still stands, whatever the circumstances. It is, in fact, a mandate which changing conditions, resources and techniques can do little to alter, since the mission to which it commits us is primarily to be the human Presence of Jesus Christ who is the same yesterday, today and forever. Our vocation is corporately to make visible his total response to God's love and truth in the terms of each distinct culture, old or new, so as to affirm, challenge, redeem and fulfil it from within, and to take the consequence of doing so with him.

Partnership for World Mission

Church Army
(International work)
Independents Road
Blackheath
London
SE3 9LG
Tel: 0181 318 1226
Registered charity number 226226

The Church's Ministry among Jewish People (CMJ)
30c Clarence Road
St Albans
Herts
AL1 4JJ
Tel: 01727 833114
Registered charity number 228519

Church Mission Society (CMS)
Partnership House
157 Waterloo Road
London SE1 8UU
Registered charity no 220297
Telephone 0171 216 1370
Registered charity number 220297

Crosslinks
251 Lewisham Way
London
SE4 1XF
Tel: 0181 691 6111
Registered charity number 249986

Intercontinental Church Society (Intercon)
175 Tower Bridge Road
London
SE1 2AQ
Tel: 0171 407 4588
Registered charity number 241111

Mid-Africa Ministry (CMS) (MAM)
Partnership House
157 Waterloo Road
London
SE1 8UU
Tel: 0171 261 1370
Registered charity number 220297

Mission to Seamen
St Michael Paternoster Royal
College Hill
London
EC4 2RL
Tel: 0171 248 5202
Registered charity number 212432

Mothers' Union
(International Work)
The Mary Sumner House
24 Tufton Street
London
SW1P 3RB
Tel: 0171 222 5533
Registered charity number 240531

South American Mission Society (SAMS)
Allen Gardiner House
12 Fox Hill
Selly Oak
Birmingham
B29 4AG
Tel: 0121 472 2616
Registered charity number 221328

The Society for Promoting Christian Knowledge worldwide
Holy Trinity Church
Marylebone Road
London
NW1 4DU
Tel: 0171 387 5282
Registered charity number 231144

United Society for the Propagation of the Gospel (USPG)
Partnership House
157 Waterloo Road
London
SE1 8XA
Tel: 0171 928 8681
Registered charity number 234518

Partnership for World Mission is a Constituent Committee of the Board of Mission and brings together the General Synod and the World Mission agencies of the Church of England. For further information contact any one of the eleven mission agency members of PWM.